Thank You Mama

A Coloring Book for Mother's Day

Welcome to "Thank You, Mama," a coloring book specially designed to celebrate the wonderful bond between a mother and her child.

This book is a heartfelt tribute to all the hardworking and nurturing moms who have tirelessly dedicated their lives to improving ours.

Mother's Day is a special occasion to show gratitude and appreciation to our moms, and this coloring book is a beautiful way to express your love and admiration for them.

With intricate designs and heartwarming sentiments, each page offers a unique opportunity to reflect on the special moments shared with our mothers.

Whether young or old, this coloring book is an excellent way to show appreciation to the most important woman in your life. Let your imagination run wild with each stroke of your coloring tools, and create something unique and memorable for your mom.

On behalf of the "Thank You Mama" team, we wish all the moms out there a Happy Mother's Day. We hope this coloring book brings you joy and helps you celebrate the love that binds you and your children together.

Happy coloring!